*Lightning
and
Ashes*

Lightning and Ashes

Poems
John Guzlowski

STEEL TOE BOOKS
BOWLING GREEN, KENTUCKY

ISBN 0 9743264 5 3 (978 0 9743264 5 0)
Cover & book Design by Joelean Copeland

Steel Toe Books
Department of English
Western Kentucky University
1906 College Heights Blvd. #11086
Bowling Green, KY 42101 1086

Contents

Part III
What the War Was Like

Epilogue

To my mother, my father, and my sister

Prologue

My Mother Reads My Poem "Cattle Train to Magdeburg"

She looks at me and says,
"That's not how it was.
I couldn't see anything
except when they stopped
the boxcars and opened the doors

And I didn't see
any of those rivers,
and if I did, I didn't know
their names. No one said,
'Look, look this river
is the Warta, and there
that's the Vistula.'

What I remember
is the bodies being
pushed out—sometimes
women would kick them out
with their feet.

Now it sounds terrible.

You think we were bad women
but we weren't. We were girls
taken from homes, alone.
Some had seen terrible things
done to their families.

Even though you're a grown man
and a teacher, we saw things
I don't want to tell you about."

Part I

What It's Like Now

My Mother Prays for Death

She is the poet of dead ends, old despairs
written in whispers, beads slipping between
her fingers like peas dropping into soup.
In her hands, the rosary is a ring of bones,
yellow as old ivory, hard as living.
Her wooden suitcase holds nothing.
She doesn't need what she leaves behind:
the empty house, the worthless bed,
the pictures she gathered over the years.

These photos are memories, and memories
belong to someone else: the daughter
who will not speak to her, the husband
who died believing in a God she can't
imagine, the foolish son who dreams
somewhere of violins, of snow falling
like soft sand on a prairie, of children
waiting for the sound of a key in a lock.

If her husband and her daughter and her son
were here now beside her in this room,
she'd ask, "Why are we born, why do we die?"
She'd say, "If you could answer these questions,
I would answer all the others." They are easy.
They come from a land of simple faces, of blue
novelty drinks topped with paper umbrellas,
of dinners that are almost never illusions.

Where she comes from, a mother's screams
last longer than a photograph, longer
than bronze shoes, and everything's lost
the way a penny's lost in the dirt at our feet.
Sorrow is the only gift God bestows.

My Mother Talks about the Slave Labor Camps

1. The Places She Lived

She has the peasants' view of the world:
Disorder and chaos, roads that end
In marshy fields, chickens that begin
To bleed from the mouth for no reason.
Nobody makes movies of such lives,
She says, and begins to tell me the story
Of when the Americans first came,
Of the sergeant who stood with a suitcase
In the yard between the barracks.

He was shouting, screaming.
They didn't know what he wanted
And feared him. One of the women
Came out (first, she hid her children
Under the bed) and then another.
They knew he wasn't a German.
When fifteen of them stood in the yard,
He opened the suitcase, emptied
Its *deutsche marks* on the ground,
Said in broken German, "This is for you,
Take it, this is the money they owe you."

And then the British soldiers came,
And put them in another camp,
Where the corpses still had not been buried,
Where the water was bad, where my mother
Got sick, where her stool was as red
As the beets she had to dig everyday.
And my father worked hard, sawing
The wood, getting ready for winter,
Like he did in Poland. He knew this work
And did it for her and the children,
My sister and me. But the British
Moved them again, to another camp,

And they had to leave the wood, even though
My father tried to carry some on his back.
And it was cold in the new place, and many
Of the babies died, and my sister was very sick,
Maybe from drinking the dirty water.

2. How Her Mother and Sister Died

Sometimes, my mother says, her home
West of Lvov comes back to her in dreams
That open in grayness with the sounds
Of a young, flowered girl in white
Singing a prayer of first communion,
The dirt streets around the church pure
With priests and girls and boys.

The singing prayer leads her to the grave
Where her mother and her sister Genja
And her sister's baby daughter lie,
The marshy grave where the hungry men
Dropped them after shooting them
And cutting them in secret places.

My mother says, these men from the east
Were like buffaloes: terrible and big.

She waves the dreams away with her hand
And starts again, talking of plowing the fields
Of cutting winter wood, of that time
When the double bladed axe slipped
And sank a wound so deep in her foot
That she felt her heart would not
Jar loose from its frozen pause.

3. What the War Taught Her

My mother learned that sex is bad,
Men are worthless, it is always cold
And there is never enough to eat.

She learned that if you are stupid
With your hands you will not survive
The winter even if you survive the fall.

She learned that only the young survive
The camps. The old are left in piles
Like worthless paper, and babies
Are scarce like chickens and bread.

She learned that the world is a broken place
Where no birds sing, and even angels
Cannot bear the sorrows God gives them.

She learned that you don't pray
Your enemies will not torment you.
You only pray that they will not kill you.

My Mother's Optimism

When she was seventy eight years old
and the angel of death called to her
and told her the vaginal bleeding
that had been starting and stopping
like a crazy menopausal period
was ovarian cancer, she said to him,
"Listen Doctor, I don't have to tell you
your job. If it's cancer it's cancer.
If you got to cut it out, you got to."

After surgery, in the convalescent home
among the old men crying for their mothers,
and the silent roommates waiting for death
she called me over to see her wound,
stapled and stitched, fourteen raw inches
from below her breasts to below her navel.
And when I said, "Mom, I don't want to see it,"
she said, "Johnny, don't be such a baby."

Six months later, at the end of her chemo,
my mother knows why the old men cry.
A few wiry strands of hair on head,
her hands so weak she can't hold a cup,
her legs swollen and blotched with blue lesions,
she says, "I'll get better. After his chemo,
Pauline's second husband had ten more years.
He was playing golf and breaking down doors
when he died of a heart attack at ninety."

Then my mom's eyes lock on mine, and she says,
"You know, optimism is a crazy man's mother."

And she laughs.

Dying in a Blue Room in Arizona

I wait for my mother to stand
and sing about the young girl
who stares into the deep well
and dreams of her lover
whose blood gives life
to the poppies on Cassino

and to call me *Johnny* again
and take my hand and dance
an arm twirling Polka the way
she did when I was six
and she could not have yet
dreamed her own dying
nor all the distances between us

I want her to tell me
Co będzię, to bezię

And I want to believe
That these words are some kind
Of grace that will free her
From this ocean of tears

Why My Mother Stayed with My Father

She knew he was worthless the first time
she saw him in the camps: his blind eye,
his small size, the way his clothes carried
the smell of the dead men who wore them before.

In America she learned he couldn't fix a leak
or drive a nail straight. He knew nothing
about the world, the way the planets moved,
the tides. The moon was just a hole in the sky,

electricity a mystery as great as death.
The first time lightning shorted the fuses,
he fell to his knees and prayed to Blessed Mary
to bring back the miracle of light and lamps.

He was a drunk too. Some Fridays he drank
his check away as soon as he left work.
When she'd see him stagger, she'd knock him down
and kick him till he wept. He wouldn't crawl away.

He was too embarrassed. Sober, he'd beg
in the bars on Division for food or rent
till even the drunks and bartenders
took pity on this dumb polack.

My father was like that, but he stayed
with her through her madness in the camps
when she searched among the dead for her sister,
and he stayed when it came back in America.

Maybe this was why my mother stayed.
She knew only a man worthless as mud,
worthless as a broken dog would suffer
with her through all of her sorrow.

Work and Death

At the end
my father sat in his garden
in the early morning

the desert in Sun City,
Arizona, this strange place,
still cool

the clear light
tinged with desert blue

the pigeons cooing.

He couldn't lift
the shovel then, drag
the bag of topsoil
from here to there.

He couldn't breathe
or stand either.
There wasn't much
left to him.

But he could nod
toward an orange tree,
its roots bound in burlap,
and point to the place
where he wanted me
to plant it.

There, he'd say
to me in Polish,
please, plant it there.

My Father Dying

His death like all death
is hard. There is no peace
in the darkness. His right eye,

the one that sees, is looking
for someone to comfort him.
He knows his mother is dead

but he whispers for her still,
the way he did as a boy
crying at her deathbed.

In his Polish the word
is three long, pleading
syllables: "*Mamusha.*"

The second syllable
is stressed, the third
falls off into silence.

Just yesterday, he talked
a little, asked for water,
smiled, when I gave him some.

But today, he can only
call for his mother. Hope is
the cancer no drug can cure.

What My Father Believed

He didn't know about the Rock of Ages
or bringing in the sheaves or Jacob's ladder
or gathering at the beautiful river
that flows beneath the throne of God.
He'd never heard of the Baltimore Catechism
either, and didn't know the purpose of life
was to love and honor and serve God.

He'd been to the village church as a boy
in Poland, and knew he was Catholic
because his mother and father were buried
in a cemetery under wooden crosses.
His sister Catherine was buried there too.

The day their mother died Catherine took
to the kitchen corner where the stove sat,
and cried. She wouldn't eat or drink, just cried
until she died there, died of a broken heart.
She was three or four years old, he was five.

What he knew about the nature of God
and religion came from the sermons
the priests told at mass, and this got mixed up
with his own life. He knew living was hard,
and that even children are meant to suffer.
Sometimes, when he was drinking he'd ask,
"Didn't God send his own son here to suffer?"

My father believed we are here to lift logs
that can't be lifted, to hammer steel nails
so bent they crack when we hit them.
In the slave labor camps in Germany,
He'd seen men try the impossible and fail.

He believed life is hard, and we should
help each other. If you see someone
on a cross, his weight pulling him down
and breaking his muscles, you should try
to lift him, even if only for a minute,
even though you know lifting won't save him.

Pigeons

My father dreams of pigeons,
their souls, their thin cradles
of bone, but it is their luck

he admires most. A boy in Poznan
in a dawn all orange and pinks,
his hands opened like a saint's

and taught those birds to fly, to rise
on the air, their wings beating
the rooftops into flesh, into dreams

of angels above the crystal trees.
And later in the gray dawn clouds
blowing about him in the camps,

where not even pigeons were safe,
where his body, thin then,
like a shoelace, sought other dreams

other bodies, and found only
the comfort of worms   even then
he could still remember

the birds without chains,
breathing quickly and cooing
"We are going, we are going."

Part II

*When My Mother and My Father,
My Sister Danusha and I Came
to America*

Displaced Persons

We came with heavy suitcases
made from boards by brothers
we left behind, came from Magdeburg
and Katowice and before that
Lvov, our mother's true home,

came with our tongues
in tatters, our teeth in our pockets,
hugging only ourselves, our bodies
stiff like frightened ostriches.

We were the orphans in ragged wool
who shuffled in line to eat or pray
or beg anyone for charity.

Remembering the air and the trees,
the sky above the Polish fields,
we dreamt only of the lives waiting
for us in Chicago and St. Louis
and Superior, Wisconsin

like pennies
in our mouths.

1. What My Father Brought with Him

He knew death the way a blind man
knows his mother's voice. He had walked
through villages in Poland and Germany

where only the old were left to search
for oats in the fields or beg the soldiers
for a cup of milk. He knew the dead,

the way they smelled and their dark full faces,
the clack of their teeth when they were desperate
to tell you of their lives. Once he watched

a woman in the moments before she died
take a stick and try to write her name
in the mud where she lay. He'd buried

children too, and he knew he could do any kind
of work a man could ask him to do.
He knew there was only work or death.

He could dig up beets and drag fallen trees
without bread or hope. The war taught him how.
He came to the States with this and his tools,

hands that had worked bricks and frozen mud
and knew the language the shit bosses spoke.

2. I Dream of My Father as He Was When He First Came Here Looking for Work

I wake up at the Greyhound Station
in Chicago, and my father stands there,
strong and brave, the young man of my poems,
a man who can eat bark and take a blow
to the head and ask you if you have more.

In each hand he holds a wooden suitcase
and I ask him if they are heavy.

He smiles, "Well, yes, naturally. They're made
of wood," but he doesn't put them down.
Then he tells me he has come from the war
but remembers little, only one story:

Somewhere in a gray garden he once watched
a German sergeant chop a chicken up
for soup and place the pieces in a pot,
everything, even the head and meatless feet.
Then he ate all the soup and wrapped the bones
in cloth for later. My father tells me,
"Remember this: this is what war is.

One man has a chicken, and another doesn't.
One man is hungry and another isn't.
One man is alive and another is dead."

I say, there must be more, and he says,
"No, that's all there is. Everything else
is the fancy clothes they put on the corpse."

3. His First Job in America

That first winter
working construction
west of Chicago
he loved the houses,
how fragile they looked,
the walls made of thin layers
of brick, the floors
just a single planking
of plywood.

A fussy, sleepy child
could destroy such a home.
It wasn't meant to witness
bombing or the work of snipers
or German 88s.

He worked there
until the cold and wind
cut him, and he found himself
thinking for hours of the way
he stacked bricks in the ruins
of Magdeburg and Berlin.

Finally, he quit
not because he was afraid
but because he knew
he could without fear

his shovel left
standing at an angle
in a pile of sand.

A Letter to My Mother from Poland, October 4, 1952

Dearest Tekla, my only sister,

The war has been over for so long but still we suffer the leavings of war. We have tables but no food, pain but no medicine, strong metal beds but no straw to sleep on.

Each day I wait for night to free me from the longing but it only brings me dreams of our dead mother crying about the wash, blaming me for the dresses I can't get clean. I hold them above the tub but haven't the strength to lower them into the water.

Sometimes, I see her standing in the doorway looking east toward the autumn forest where snow already falls. Perhaps if you could come back to Poland and travel back to the village with me, maybe we could find the grave where they dropped her and Genja and Genja's baby. Someone there must know where they are buried. Maybe then mother would stop coming to me.

If you could come in the spring, perhaps you could bring me a bolt of blue cloth, blue with little white flowers. You know the kind we wore the year before the war. A new dress for summer would be so nice.

Your loving sister,

Sophia

Stories My Sister Danusha Told Me

1. Poor Adas

Adas is sad.
His father is dead.
His mother works hard
but she makes very little.

Adas always
comes to school
in worn out clothes
and he is always hungry.

He doesn't have money
to buy books or pencils

But the good children
don't forget about Adas.

They share
their bread with him
and sometimes

they buy him a pencil.

God loves these children
and He loves their parents too.

2. Sweet Little Birds

Hungry birds
sit on the window sill
and look in.

The good children
stop playing with their dolls
and red balls and rubber trucks

and they open the window
and give the birds some bread.

They will never forget.

3. The Storm

The storm clouds
hide the heavens
and the thunder is loud,
and black and green clouds
roll toward the children.

The sparrows hide in trees
or under the eves of roofs.

The children run from the garden
where they have been watering
the beautiful red flowers.

They fear the flash of lightning
and the way it strikes the trees
but their grandmother tells them
not to cry because "God watches
over good children and sparrows,
and soon the storm will end
and the sun will shine again."

Dumb Polacks

Good children, we played outside
while our tired mother slept inside
resting from working the night shift,
and then a boy came along.

A bully, he was big and hard
and threw the ball at us
again and again, and called us DPs
and Dumb Polacks. Frightened

we called to our mother softly
in the English we didn't know
and had only practiced in whispers,
"Mother, Mother, Mother."

She had no English at all
and didn't come, and the boy
kicked us 'til we both were screaming,
"Mother, Mother, Mother."

Back in the house later,
with our tears and fearfulness,
we told her what happened
and she said, "Why didn't you call?"

We just stood there in silence.
What could we say to her?

Whistling

My mother always said whistling
in the house whistles the devil in.

Even if you whistle low, you'll hear
his knuckles nicking on the door,

hollow like the sound a pig's snout
makes knocking against the bucket

that holds its slop. You'll hear
his knock even if you whistle

like a happy child sitting
near a stove reading comics.

Nothing will keep the devil out,
she says. Even if you pray to Jesus

you'll hear Satan's wooden knock
or feel him smiling in the cloud

of dark stars inside your head
when you try to sleep in your bed.

A Young Soldier from Czestochowa

In his dreams
my father cradles
the boy in his arms

his skin is white
already

his arms gone
at the shoulders

his blood
on the dreamer's
hands and face

My father wipes it
from the boy's eyes
And holds him
closer

Fussy Eaters

Fifty years later, my mother says,
Johnny, remember how you wouldn't eat
the good Polish sausage your father brought
from Starchek's Deli? Such a fussy eater

and Danusha was worse. In the camps,
she would chew on a stick from morning
to night and beg on her knees to get
some of the breast milk I was saving for you

because the doctor said you were a goner.
Not till I came to America did I understand
what he meant by this word. A goner—yes.
But in America, Danusha wouldn't eat

the sweet cabbage with vinegar and onions
or the dumplings cooked with hot butter.
Only ten, she'd look me hard in the eyes—
like I was a stone dropped from the sky—

and say, I can't eat this Polack food.
It's gray and tough and laced with veins that steal
my breath away so much I feel like choking.
And I would say to her, But you'd eat

marzipani, and one time I slapped her
and gave her five dollars—this in a time
when you'd work hard all day for five dollars—
and she went to Rickey's Restaurant

and ate meatloaf and mashed potatoes
and came home and was sick in the toilet.
This made me happy, and I said to her,
Now, you'll eat my cooking. Now, you'll like it.

Danusha

Do you remember those Sundays
Driving with mother and father
In that big gray Desoto to the bars
On the prairie north of Chicago?

You asked me, your little brother,
To dance to Hank Williams singing,
"Hey, good looking, Whatcha got cooking?"
And we twirled and jitterbugged,
Waltzed and stepped beneath the blue
And green Christmas tree lights.

Did the drunks turn from their dreams
Of Normandy with its gray sands
And the Ardennes with its frozen dead
To watch us dance the way they danced
When they were children before the war?
Did they know that we were DPs,
The children they fought in Remagen
To free? Did they turn and clap,
Toss us nickels and mercury head dimes?
And what did we talk about as we danced?

I'm sure it wasn't about the way
Mother slapped you across your face,
Chased you screaming through the rooms,
Or swung for you under the bed
With the broken broomstick handle.

Listen, I am thinking of you still
And praying that you forgive me
For never telling you that I knew
How bad she hurt you
And if there was some way
I could dance with you again

Beneath those blue and green lights
I would, and I would beg you
In my broken Polish not to cry.

Prosze Danousha,
Prosze nie plakach.

Chores

One day I asked my mother,
"How about an allowance
for sweeping these stairs?
A quarter once a week?"

My mother gave me a hard look
and told me in the old country
kids slaughtered pigs on their own
with wooden hammers and drained

the black lumpy blood
from the carcasses and made
Polish sausage from the guts
every day of the week

for nothing, not even a quick
thanks a lot in Polish.
And then she said to me,
"If you won't do the chores

unless I pay you, then don't."
And she grabbed my broom,
and went outside and stopped
the first kid she saw on the street,

a kid I hated from school,
and she gave him a quarter
just for doing the stairs
I would've done for free.

Poland

They'll never see it again, these old Poles
with their dreams of Poland. My father
told me when I was a boy that those who tried
in '45 were turned back at the borders

by shoeless Russians dressed in rags and riding
shaggy ponies. The Poles fled through the woods,
the unlucky ones left behind, dead
or what's worse wounded, the lucky ones

gone back to wait in the old barracks
in the concentration and labor camps
in Gatersleben or Wildflecken
for some miracle that would return them

to Poznan or Katowice. But God
wasn't listening or His hands were busy
somewhere else. Later, in America
these Poles gathered with their brothers

and with their precious sons and daughters
every May 3, Polish Constitution Day,
to pray for the flag. There was no question
then what the colors stood for, red for all

that bleeding sorrow, white for innocence.
And always the old songs telling the world
Poland would never fall so long as poppies
flower red, and flesh can conquer rock or steel.

Refugees never learn what their children
always learn. Those left behind in Poland
left the past behind. Borders stay open
only in the dreams of those dying on this side,

And dying at last of liver cancer, my father
couldn't sing those old songs. Did he dream
of those borders? It would be nice to say
he did, but I only saw confusion in his eyes.

My Father's Prayer

Dear Baby Jesus,
If You have any pity left
bestow it, please, on my wife.
She suffers from the war.

You know about her mother,
and her sister and the baby,
and about the things
she's told no one.

Me? I have my whiskey,
and the fighting.

When my sorrow is great
I go to the taverns
on Division Street
and drink and fight
with the Americans,
men who are bigger
and harder than me.

I thank them
for beating me
till I can't remember
the sorrow.

But my wife Tekla—
she is one of your sparrows
and the pain she feels
has nowhere to go
so she beats our daughter
sweet Danusha
and is cruel to our son
who she also loves.

My wife's a good woman
but like all of us
she has seen
terrible things.

Here's What My Mother Won't Talk About

Just a girl of nineteen
with the grace of flowers
in her hair

coming home
from the pastures
beyond the woods
where the cows drift
slowly, through a twilight
of dust, warm and still
as August

She finds her mother
a bullet in her throat
her sister's severed breasts
in the dust by her feet
the dead baby
still in its blanket

It all ends there
not in the camps
but there

Ask her

She'll wave her hand
tell you you're a fool
tell you

if they give you bread
eat it

if they beat you
run

Part III

What the War Was Like

There Were No Miracles

Men died where they stood

Children were left
for the dogs and the pigs

Schoolgirls came home
to find their mothers dead
their fathers with necks cut

Priests sat at their tables
wondering if they should
kill themselves

Some of them did

Others hid in the woods
till hunger and fear
brought them back
to the villages
and the trains
that would take them
to death

and some took their crosses
with them

and others left them
in the stations
where they'd prayed
for miracles.

German Soldiers Come to My Mother's Village

On their knees, and one by one, each man
and woman, each child, is shot and falls
backward without a sound into the mud
like an iron rod. God doesn't love these people.

They live in darkness, thatch their low cottages
with straw, burn wet wood in mud stoves
like evil children in a fairy tale.

There is no fat for their lamps. The sole light
you see comes from a candle in a cellar
where a woman in rags searches for roots.

This is the only world they'll ever know:
these huts, and the mud road that brought us here
and will take us out again when we are done.
This is where we gather them, here on this road.

Listening to their screams and pleading
we know these people will never again
drink from their pond or make shoes of straw
or eat a filling meal of sausage and bread
or laugh like children laugh alone in the dark.

We soldiers are only human. We love
to kill. It is the hidden God in each of us.

My Mother's Neighbors

Their clothes are wet and cold with the blood
of the baby and the women they killed
in the barn. But they won't remember that.

They'll only remember this walk home, the snow
falling fast around them, muting the clicking trees
and silencing the birds. They will remember

their slow talk, the old men going on about
how the potatoes they gathered this year
could never match the weight of last year's harvest

the young men trying to hide their joy
by whispering about the village girls
and what they have seen beneath their dresses.

Later they will all be home. Already their wives
and mothers watch for them at the windows,
afraid the snow will catch them far from home.

Cattle Train to Magdeburg

My mother still remembers

The long train to Magdeburg
the box cars
bleached gray
by Baltic winters

The rivers and the cities
she had never seen before
and would never see again:
the sacred Vistula
the smoke haunted ruins of Warsaw
the Warta, where horse flesh
met steel and fell

The leather fists
of pale boys
boys her own age
perhaps seventeen
perhaps nineteen
but different
convinced of their godhood
by the cross they wore
different from the one
she knew in Lvov

The long twilight journey
to Magdeburg—
four days that became six years
six years that became sixty

And always a train of box cars
bleached to Baltic gray.

My Father Talks about the Boxcars

The train would slow, and then stop
And we would wait for the doors
To grind open so we could see
Where we were, and sometimes

There would be children in the fields
Bent over boards or a broken plow
And we would beg them for water
And they would say, "Dear Jesus,

If we only could, but the Germans
Would shoot us," and we would beg
The children to tell us where we were
And we'd ask if they knew where

The tracks led—and they'd whisper,
The tracks went west to Germany
And maybe further but they didn't know,
Maybe to America or France.

And we would watch the doors
Grind back and close with hungry eyes.

Grief

My mother cried for a week, first in the boxcars
then in the camps. Her friends said, "Tekla,
don't cry, the Germans will shoot you
and leave you in the field," but she couldn't stop.

Even when she had no more tears, she cried,
cried the way a dog will gulp for air
when it's choking on a stick or some bone
it's dug up in a garden and swallowed.

The woman in charge gave her a cold look
and knocked her down with her fist like a man,
and then told her if she didn't stop crying
she would call the guard to stop her crying.

But my mother couldn't stop. The howling
was something loose in her nothing could stop.

Hunger in the Labor Camps

1. What My Father Ate

He ate what he couldn't eat,
what his mother taught him not to:
brown grass, small chips of wood, the dirt
beneath his gray dark fingernails.

He ate the leaves off trees. He ate bark.
He ate the flies that tormented
the mules working in the fields.
He ate what would kill a man

in the normal course of his life:
leather buttons, cloth caps, anything
small enough to get into his mouth.
He ate roots. He ate newspaper.

In his slow clumsy hunger
he did what the birds did, picked
for oats or corn or any kind of seed
in the dry dung left by the cows.

And when there was nothing to eat
he'd search the ground for pebbles
and they would loosen his saliva
and he would swallow that.
And the other men did the same.

2. What a Starving Man Has

He has his skin. He has a thinness
to his eyes no bread will ever redeem.
He has no belly and his long muscles
stand out in relief as if they'd been flayed.

He is a bony mule with the hard eyes
one encounters in nightmares or in hell,
and he dreams of cabbage and potatoes
the way a boy dreams of women's breasts.

They come uncalled for, round and fevered
like rain that will never stop. There is always
the empty sea in his belly, rising
falling and seeking land, and next to him

there's always another starving man who says,
"Help me, Brother. I am dying here."

3. Among Sleeping Strangers

The moon set early and it grew darker,
and the men settled to sleep in the cold
without blankets. Soon it would be spring
but it was still cold, and it was always cold

at night, and they did what men always did
at night when they were cold. They pressed their bodies
together and looked for warmth the way a man
who has nothing will look, expecting nothing

and thankful to God for the little he finds,
and the night was long as it always was
and some men crawled roughly across the others
to reach an outside wall to relieve themselves,

and some men started coughing and the coughing
entered the dreams of some of the other men
and they remembered the agony
of their mothers and grandfathers dying

of hunger or cholera, their lungs coughed up
in blood streaked phlegm, and some men dreamt
down deeper and deeper against the cold
till they came somehow to that holy moment

in the past when they were warm and full
and loved, and the sun in those dreams rose early
and set late and the days were full of church bells
and the early spring flowers that stirred their lives

and in the morning the men shook away
from the cold bodies of their brothers
and remembered everything they had lost,
their wives and sisters, their lovers, their homes

their frozen fingers, their fathers, the soil
they'd been born on, the souls they'd been born with,
and then they crawled up out of the earth
and gathered together to work in the dawn.

4. The Germans

These men belonged to the Germans
the way a mule belonged to the Germans
and the Germans stood watching

their hunger and then their deaths,
watched them as if they were dead trees
in the wind, and waited for them to fall,

and some of the men did. They sank
to their knees like children begging
forgiveness for sins they couldn't recall,

or they failed to rise when the others did
and were left in the wet gray fields
where the Germans watched them

and the Germans stood watching
when the men who were still hungry
came back and lifted the dead men

and carried their thin bones to the barn,
and buried them there before eating the soup
that wouldn't have kept them alive.

The Germans knew a starving man
needed more than soup and more than bread
but still they stood and watched.

The Work He Did in Germany

He lifts the shovel, sees the dirt,
the clods still heavy with snow,
and knows that this will always
be his life, one shovel and then
another shovel until his arms
are shaking. He never knows

what the guards will say to him.
Maybe they'll ask him for a song
he knew in Poland that he sang
while leading the steaming cows
into the woods early in the spring.
And he will smile and sing

and ask them if they'd like another.
Or maybe they will tell him
he is a fool and his mother
a pig the farm boys fuck
when their own hands are weak
from pulling on their sore meat.

And my father will shovel
in terror and think of the words
he will not say: Sirs, we are all
brothers, and if this war ever ends,
please, never tell your children
what you've done to me today.

My Father Tells a Story

My friend Jashu was an artist in Wilno
before the war. He would paint pictures
of young women in dresses made of roses
and yellow flowers no one had ever seen.

In the camp he would push a stick
through the dust and sketch your face
give you eyes like Charlie Chaplin
or a funny stomach like Oliver Hardy.

Jashu told me of the women he knew
before the war, of making love in blue rooms
after a dessert of marzipani on silver plates,
then going into the dark, wet park

And making love again in the half shelter
of a band shell or kiosk. Near the end
he told me he had the French disease,
and when I said I didn't understand

he pointed down to his thing there
and asked me what he should do.
He was a good friend, and I looked him
in the eye and said, "Go to the Elbe

And drown yourself." He laughed and went
to Stefan Czernak who said, "Go to the Germans
And tell them what you did." The Germans asked,
"Who was the woman you made love to?"

He told them, and they beat her with clubs
and killed her and they beat him too,
and castrated him, and killed him.

Worthless

My mother looks at herself
in her dress and striped coat
and knows she is who she is—
bones and skin, and the war
has always been here with her,

like an older brother, not mean
or evil but hard, never soft, teaching
hesitance and patience, teaching her
not to put her hand out to take
the cup of water or touch the bread.

It has always been this way
and will always be this way.
War has no beginning, no end.
War is the god who breeds and kills.

The Third Winter of War: Buchenwald

Prologue:

His hands are cut into pieces,
each piece small, pebble size.

If you are hungry at night,
You'll put a piece in your mouth.

I.

He dreams about fires and bricks,
a church he saw in Warsaw
after the bombers pulled it apart
and broke it up, and smashed it
and left it bleeding and praying
for death the way a woman
in labor will pray when she knows
nothing will save the baby
waiting in her womb to be born.

II.

Sometimes at night, the guards tell him
to milk the cows. He smiles and nods.

The cow's hair is soft, like his mother's,
and warm as a stove steaming on a gray
winter morning.
                    The mud and shit
around the cows are warm too.

In the dark, he raises his cupped hands,
drinks the milk, and knows there'll be more,
and knows too the guards will club him
when they smell the milk on his lips.

III.

He is swimming in a dark river.

Above his head there is a moon
as big as a theater he once saw
in Magdeburg, but there is no light.

The moon is a bright place in the sky
but none of the light falls on him
or his journey's path.

                He remembers
he cannot swim and begins falling
without struggling, deeper and deeper
into the black water.

                Nothing
will save him. He knows this and wakes
waiting to dream of the river's bottom.

IV.

The bricks of the burning city are hot.
He doesn't have to touch them to know this.
Everywhere he looks, Germans stand away
from the bricks, stand with their hands raised

as if to keep the city's death at bay.
Even where the dying shout and plead
under the hot bricks, Germans stand this way.
They stand in the middle of the street.

It's not important who is under the bricks.
It could be a soldier or a child, a mother
or one of the slaves forced like him to dig
with his hands under the bricks for the dead.

The Germans don't want to know who is under
the hot bricks. When a thing is truly bad,
you can do nothing to change it. You must
stand away from it—hands raised to heaven.

V.

He feels trees are growing in him,
their roots hardening into bone,
the bone growing into stone,
the stone hardening into iron,

and the iron in turn hardening
into steel and more sorrow.

What is the blood in his heart?

VI.

Beyond the field and the guards,
he sees a witch in the pine trees
dancing in rags, the snow a veil,

the witch twirling like a girl
in a spring world of greens and blues
so rich not even a holy man

would turn away, a witch twirling
her arms above her head, her breasts
fat as pillows, warm as fresh milk,

singing a child's song about cows
coming home from the happy fields
and the pretty girls who lead them,

singing a song to Jesus and Mary
His mother who hears our prayers
and beseeches Him to hear them too.

VII.

He remembers a movie he once saw
when he escaped from the camp.

In it, one of the heroes is a fat man,
the other skinny. On a boat lost at sea,
they look at each other in hunger and cry.

Then fatty smiles, and skinny cries harder.

VIII.

He dreams he's one of the boy scouts
of Katowice, forced to jump
by the Nazis from the tower
in the park. He falls screaming.

His courage will not give him wings.

His dead mother watches and cries.
Waking, he remembers her love
for him and how he cried
when she died in the winter.

Her love couldn't give her wings

IX.

He dreams about a revolution,
a city on a black hill destroyed by fire
and sword, by winged soldiers diving
through the sky on winged horses.

X.

He is as hungry as a dog in winter
in a forest filled with so much snow
that all the woodsmen and their wives
and children have fled to the village.

Only the tips of the highest pine trees
peak out, their needles pointed east
ready for spring's first light to shine.

XI.

He dreams about men whose hands
change color, from yellow and black,
to white and green, the men staring
at their rainbow hands and whistling
like boys calling dogs.
                        The change
doesn't frighten them, but they worry
about what their fathers and mothers
will say when they come home,
old with hands like rainbows.

XII.

He lies on a shelf at night and thinks
of milk and oranges, sausage
and chicken breasts, his mother's bread,
brown and warm, boiled dumplings
filled with sauerkraut, dumplings
filled with soft cheese, dumplings
filled with plums and sweet cherries,
and all of them pitted and perfect.

He knows he never again has to worry
about breaking his teeth on the pits.

His teeth were left in the frozen mud
where the guard hit him with the club.

XIII.

He dreams dogs change into men
and sit at a table to discuss the war,
why it began and how it will end.

He wants to ask the dogs a question
but they can't understand his howling.

XIV.

He wishes he could shit turds
as soft and pure as a baby's.

XV.

Beneath the skin on his arms,
he sees stones growing, pressing
against his skin, trying to burst through.

He pushes them down, but the pain
in his arms is terrible, violent,
like a burning no one can stop.

Crying like a fool, he tries
to pull the stones out, digs his fingers
deeper into his bones for the stones
that pull deeper and deeper down.

XVI.

He dreams a comedy—men lifting
heavy wooden trunks onto a cart
and slipping in manure, rising
again and then slipping again.

This goes on until their faces,
hands and clothes are covered
in brown and green and yellow.

He laughs until someone kicks him.

XVII.

His urine is soapy, the color
of wheat, and there is always pain
when he pees.
       He watches it like
a man on an island watches the tides.

XVIII.

He wakes in the night in the barracks,
his sweat cold among the dying.

He knows there are thieves all around
who will steal his wooden shoes
and the belt that keeps his pants up
and the bread he hides at his groin.

These thieves are like his brothers,
but at night loneliness and sorrow
will turn your brother against you.

XIX.

He smiles tonight because the shelf
he sleeps on in the barn gives off
the hot, wet smell of boiled potatoes.

XX.

He dreams he's been forced to dress
the body of a woman who drowned
in the creek near his home in Poland
but her body keeps falling off
the slab where the guards dropped her.

XXI.

He dreams about men becoming
talking animals, dogs and horses,
cows and lions, and even creatures

he's never seen but only heard of,
the elephant and the gorilla,
the hippopotamus and the zebra.

He dreams again his hands are cut
to pieces. He dreams he is falling.
He dreams he is an old woman
eating the fingers of a young boy
who died when his horse reared up
crazily and crushed him.

He dreams he swims in a river
he can't escape. It is the blood
of the devil, thick and dark
and like acid to the tongue.

XXII.

Working among the bricks, lifting
them in his hands and throwing them
into the wooden cart behind him,
his body first feels hot and then
cold with the sickness and the snow.

He fears his bones will freeze and crack
the way the limbs of a tree will crack
when winter is so hard it can kill
a dog, and even kill a man.

XXIII.

He dreams of eating human flesh,
of women copulating with corpses,
of dogs licking his fingers,
of soldiers spreading manure
around the red and white roses
beside the church in his village.

XXIV.

The Germans are pulling him apart
and rushing him to the furnace.

They are like devils and the heat
burns the hair from his face.

He struggles but they beat him
with black snaking whips.
                              The wind
around his head swirls with the sound
of the whipping and the cutting.

XXV.

He dreams he is in a blue house
that collapses every night
as if the strongest wind God
ever imagined sought out
this very house every night
and pulled its iron nails loose.

XXVI.

He recalls talking with two priests
when he was just a boy. They walked
with him among the pines and held
his hands gently, told him, "There's hope

but there is also waiting. Hope
will come but waiting is the road
upon which it travels and it travels
so slowly. Till then, remember

the faith you were born to, no matter
what you are told and no matter
how much life seems to fail you,
no matter how much you fail life."

XXVII.

This is the winter that will not end,
the winter that leaves the cows frozen
in the snow, frozen in the smell
of swirling cordite from the shells—

The winter that will never end.

XXVIII.

He is the corpse without lips
or the desire to lick its lips.

He is the corpse that doesn't envy
the sparrows or the pigeons,
or the horses or cows that stand
around waiting for men to beat them
across the flanks when they're angry
or across the eyes and mouth
when the men are truly mad.

He is the corpse that has made
its journey and now waits only
for the slumber promised by God
in the bible and other books that lie.

Epilogue:

If he plants his cut off hands in the ground
will they take root, bring him the promise
of his mother and father, will a stem
grow from his wrist, leaves from his fingers,

will these be his children, will he know
how to water them, will his water be
enough to bring them the love they'll seek
as they uncurl like roses before the spring sun,

will his tears be the holy, saving water,
or will they be a blasphemy against
his blessed lord, just the bitterness
of a cow disappointed with its field?

The Beets

My mother tells me of the beets she dug up
In Germany. They were endless, redder
Than roses gone bad in an early frost,
Redder than a grown man's kidney or heart.

The first beet she remembers,
She was alone in the field, alone
Without her father or mother near,
No sister even. They were all dead,
Left behind in Lvov. The ground was wet
And cold, but not soft, never soft.

She ate the raw beet, even though
She knew they would beat her.

She says, sometimes she pretended
She was deaf, stupid, crippled,
Or diseased with Typhus or cholera,
Even with what the children called
The French disease, anything to avoid

The slap, the whip across her back
The leather fist in her face above her eye.
If she could've given them her breasts
To suck, her womb to penetrate
She would have, just so they would not
Hurt her the way they hurt her sister
And her mother and the baby.

She wonders what was her reward
For living in such a world? It was not love
Or money. She can't even remember
What happened to the *deutsche marks*
The American sergeant left that day
In the spring when the war ended.

She wonders if God will remember
Her labors. She wonders if there is a God.

Pieta in a Bombed Church, Magdeburg

My father remembers the church at midnight,
the church at dawn, altars and crosses
in shadows, a statue of a mother holding
the body of the man who was her son,
his wounds chiseled deep and cold, like mouths
hardened into stone by pain and death.

The mother and son are the color of clay
before it hardens in the kiln, the color
of the body seen on the doctor's table
or left dying in a field by soldiers.
The son looks at her face, as if he can't
turn away from her sorrow, a sorrow
she shows even in the way she holds
her head. It's clear to my father she knows
pain and how pain is like the night that never
seems to end, but finally does sometimes,
suddenly like the first of winter's frosts.

My father's memories of his own mother
are few but holy: her standing near the stove,
her sitting in the doorway with the warmth
of the sun on her face. Her hand holding
his while she probes his palm with a needle
to get the sliver out, his palm swollen,
a blister filled with pus where the sliver
waits for her needle. He feared the pain
the needle would bring, and there was pain
when she probed, and pain when she withdrew
the sliver, and pain when she pressed the fire
to his palm to burn the wound clean of poison,
but he knew she wouldn't hurt him and the pain
would be there only for a minute, and then
it would stop the greater pain inside it.

Awake already, he doesn't open his eyes.
The room's filled with the sounds of hungry men
sleeping, their groans and the waking whispers
that might be threats or prayers. Enslaved men
never sleep soundly. They dream of sorrow
and food, and the distance between them
and the ones they love, the mothers who wait
beside stoves, the fathers who sleep in their graves.

His Dead Eye

My father didn't know why he didn't die
when they clubbed him for eating the soup.

For a long time he wasn't there or anywhere,
and when he came to, his left eye was dead,
dead and open and would always stay open,
with a scar running curved and deep
from this left eye to a place above his ear.

Sometimes at night, pain would shake him awake,
and he would pray to Jesus through his fear
until he fell asleep. Sometimes, he felt the pain
during the day too, and he'd grow angry
with the men and women in the labor camp
who were like his brothers and sisters
over things they all knew didn't matter,
like shoeing a horse or clearing bricks
or bracing a barn's collapsing wall.

Later in Chicago looking for work
in some factory on Armitage Street,
my father wasn't hired once because the boss
couldn't face the scar and the dead, staring eye.

When my father died the undertaker fixed
the scar with putty and sewed the eye shut.

Night in the Labor Camp

Through the nearest window
he stares at the sky and thinks
of his dead father and mother,
his dead sister and brother,

his dead aunt and dead uncle,
his dead friend Jashu, and the boy
whose name he didn't know
who died in his arms, and all

the others who wait for him
like the first light of the sun
and the work he has to do
when the sun wakes him.

He hates no one, not God,
not the dead who come to him,
not the Germans who caught him,
not even himself for being alive.

He is a man held together
with stitches he laced himself.

In the Spring the War Ended

For a long time the war was not in the camps.
My father worked in the fields and listened
to the wind moving the grain, or a guard
shouting a command far off, or a man dying.

But in the fall, my father heard the rumbling
whisper of American planes, so high, like
angels, cutting through the sky, a thunder
even God in Heaven would have to listen to.

At last, one day he knew the war was there.
In the door of the barracks stood a soldier,
an American, short like a boy and frightened,
and my father marveled at the miracle of his youth

and took his hands and embraced him and told him
he loved him and his mother and father,
and he would pray for all his children
and even forgive him the sin of taking so long.

Epilogue

How Early Fall Came This Year

Between the rows
of tomato plants
shrunken in their cages
and cannis bulbs
buried in the snow
my daughter follows me

asks me at last
why I wear a coat
without buttons
shoes without laces

I tell her I'm a fool
in a dream of magic

drop to my knees
like a penitent seal

and while she laughs
I make up more
tell her the buttons
were stirred into soup
the laces when sold
bought the secret of bread

she doesn't need to know
my thoughts are always
with my father and mother,
dying of the blood
that survived the camps
the memories of the baby
left in the field
with the beets

the real magic

only six she'd understand
their gray voices as I did
shaping a world out of
lightning and ashes.

My Parents

My father Jan Guzlowski was born outside of Poznan in Poland in 1920. By the time he was 5 years old he was an orphan, and he and his older brother Roman went to live with his aunt and his uncle on a small farm, outside a village north of Poznan.

My mother Tekla Hanczarek was born in 1922 west of Lvov in eastern Poland. Her father was a forest ranger and her family lived in a log house in a deep woods.

Before the war, my father imagined that he would always stay on his aunt's small farm. He would take care of the pigs and the two cows. He would live according to the seasons as farmers had always lived. In spring, he would help plant the crops, the potatoes and cabbages, and take care of the new born pigs and calves. In the fall, he would help harvest the crops or slaughter one of the animals so they would have food in the winter. What little money they made, they used for buying clothes or maybe tools for the work on the farm.

He imagined that he would always live according to the seasons and the holy days that came regularly like the ringing of church bells from the steeple of the small church in the village nearby. He would put on the blue suit his uncle gave him when he turned 16 and wash and shave and go to church. A good Catholic boy, he loved going to the church on Holy Saturday to have the eggs and butter, the salt and bread blessed by the priest. My father loved going early to church on Easter Sunday, leaving the farm in the wagon even before the sun was a pink silence over the east, and coming to the church where the little girls stood in their white dresses holding the lilies while the boys seemed serious and awkward in their older brothers' suits. And there was May Day when they pledged themselves to Mary, the mother of Jesus, and then Pentecost when he imagined the tongues burning above the heads of the apostles, and Christmas with its mysterious midnight mass that began in darkness and ended in light, and the feast of the three kings and more. My father imagined that this would always be the life he lived.

My mother grew up in a deep woods 30 miles west of Lvov. She always thought she would stay in the woods where her father was a forest ranger, where they lived in a big house made of logs.

She loved the woods. She loved picking mushrooms in the spring and even when she was little she was able to tell the ones that were safe from the ones that weren't. She loved climbing the tall white birch trees in the summer when her chores in the kitchen and the garden were done. She loved to ride her pet pig Caroline in the woods or sit with her and watch the leaves fall in the autumn. She felt that Caroline the pig was smarter than her brothers Wladyu and Jan, but not as smart as Genja, her sister who was married and had a beautiful baby girl.

My mother loved to sing. There was a song about a chimney sweeper that she would sing over and over; and when her father heard it, he sometimes laughed and said, "Tekla, you're going to grow up to marry a chimney sweep, and you're cheeks will always be dusty from his dusty kisses if you keep singing that song." But she didn't care if he teased her.

She loved the song—that one about the chimney sweep and the other one about the deep well. She loved to sing about the young girl who stood by the deep well waiting for her lover, a young soldier, to come back from the wars. She had never had a boyfriend, she wasn't yet 18 and her mother said she was too young to think of boys, but Tekla didn't care. She loved the song and sometimes imagined that she was the young girl waiting for the soldier to come back from the war.

And then all that world ended when the Second World War started and the Nazis invaded Poland in September 1939. The whole world was turned upside down. Poland had a population of about 36 million at that time, and almost 6 million Jewish and Catholic Poles were killed in death camps, and almost 4 million Poles were sent to slave labor camps in Germany and the Soviet Union. My parents were sent to the ones in Germany.

In 1940 when my father was 20 he was captured during a round up. It was a Saturday, and he had walked to the village to buy some rope. The Nazi soldiers surrounded the village and took him and the other men to Germany. He stayed there for 11 years. He spent five years as a slave laborer, working in the factories and farms of the Buchenwald Concentration District. Once he escaped to some town whose name he never found out, and he hid in a movie theater where he watched silent comedies with Laurel and Hardy until the Gestapo came and arrested him and beat him and took him back. After the Americans came and the war ended, he spent 6 years as a Displaced Person, a DP, a refugee without a country who was not allowed back to Poland. He never saw his aunt or uncle or their children again.

In 1942, my mother was taken to Germany during a round up. She stayed there for 9 years. She spent 3 years there as a slave laborer, and 6 years after the war as a Displaced Person, a DP. She never saw the log house or her mother or father or the woods again.

My parents met in 1944, the year before the war ended. In 1951, my parents, my sister, and I came to the United States as Displaced Persons.

When I was home with my parents as a child growing up, I never thought much about where they came from, or where I came from. Or what their experiences had been in the war. My neighborhood in Chicago around Humboldt Park was full of people who had survived the war, Jews who crawled out of Auschwitz or lost a hand in the Warsaw Ghetto uprising, Polish Cavalry officers who still dreamed of their horses, Ukrainians who had been captured in the fighting around Stalingrad and forced to walk a thousand miles in rags to get to Germany where the soup was so bad that they called it Hitler's secret weapon.

When I was growing up, my mother never talked about the experiences she had as a young girl in Poland or in Germany, but my father did. When he had had a few drinks, he would always start talking about the war, the terrible things he had seen. But the stories he told didn't make much of an impression on me. I must have been hearing them for years. They became the white background noise of my life.

Then when I left home and went away to graduate school, I started thinking about my parents, and their lives in Germany and Poland, and thinking about these one hot afternoon in Indiana, I wrote the first of my Polish poems, "Dreams of Warsaw." And then I wrote the other poems.

Acknowledgements

I would like to thank the following for publishing some of the poems from *Lightning and Ashes*:

Atlanta Review: "Letter from Poland"

Biblioteka Slaska: Jezyk Mulow/Language of Mules "Cattle Train to Magdeburg," "Displaced Persons," "My Mother Talks About the Slave Labor Camps," and "Pigeons"

Blood to Remember: An Anthology of American Poets on the Holocaust, first edition: "Cattle Train to Magdeburg" and "How Early Fall Came This Year"

Blood to Remember, 2nd Edition: "How Early Fall Came This Year," "Hunger in the Labor Camps," "Night in the Labor Camp," and "What the War Taught My Mother"

Crab Orchard Review: "Hunger in the Labor Camps" and "Poland"

Finishing Line Press: "The Third Winter of War: Buchenwald" (Chapbook)

Madison Review: "Here's What My Mother Won't Talk About"

Margie: An American Journal of Poetry: "Looking for Work in America"

Nimrod International: "The Work He Did in Germany"

Poetry East: "Why My Mother Stayed with my Father"

Proteus: A Journal of Thought: "My Mother Reads 'Cattle Train to Magdeburg'"

The Scream on Line: "My Sister Danusha" and "Optimism"

Snake Nation Review: "The Men in the Boxcars"

Spoon River Poetry Review: "Grief," "Displaced Persons," "Fussy Eaters," "Work and Death," "My Father Dying," "Kitchen Polish," "My Mother Talks About the Slave Labor Camps," and "Pigeons"